THE FINGER LAKES

THE FINGER LAKES

Photography by
John Francis McCarthy
and
Linda Bishop McCarthy

Foreword by
Conrad T. Tunney

SKYLINE
PRESS

Our special thanks are due to Walter H. Long, Director of the Cayuga
Museum of Art and History, to Stephen Erskine, Librarian of the Seymour
Public Library, Auburn, to the Corning Museum of Glass, to the George
Eastman House and to Genesee Country Museum for their cooperation
and permission to use certain images in this book. The many private
individuals who have similarly helped us are too numerous to mention
personally but to them also we extend our thanks.

JOHN FRANCIS McCARTHY
LINDA BISHOP McCARTHY

Produced by Boulton Publishing Services Inc., Toronto
Designed by Fortunato Aglialoro

© 1984 Oxford University Press (Canadian Branch)
SKYLINE PRESS is a registered imprint of the Oxford University Press

ISBN 0-19-540608-7
2 3 4 - 7 6 5
Printed in Hong Kong by Scanner Art Services, Inc., Toronto

FOREWORD

I n writing a foreword for this book I have only one regret, that our old friend George Train, who was for over twenty years the President of the Finger Lakes Association, is no longer here to compose the foreword with me. He would have told of more than nine decades during which he enjoyed the endless bounties and pleasures of the Finger Lakes. Instead it is left to me to mention, however briefly, our vineyard-covered hills, our sparkling spring-fed lakes, our sprawling valleys and tumbling waterfalls, our noble buildings and historic cities, our well-tended farmlands and magnificent estates. Most important of all, I should speak of our fellow citizens here, nearly two million of them, many of whom can trace their ancestry back to the Revolutionary War; a friendly people, who take pride and pleasure in sharing; a rugged, reliable, independent people, with a record of hospitality second to none. Generations of such people have made of the Finger Lakes a treasure unique in the world. This book is a tribute to them and their region.

CONRAD T. TUNNEY

Executive Director,
The Finger Lakes Association
Penn Yan, New York, January 1984

INTRODUCTION

The story of New York State's Finger Lakes is one of the most colorful chapters in American history. According to the Smithsonian Institution's 'Bulletin (#30) on American Ethnology' (Sept. 1912), the northern Iroquois tribes, consisting of the Mohawks, the Oneidas, the Onondagas, the Cayugas, the Senecas, and the Tuscaroras, were second to no other Indian people north of Mexico in their political organization, statecraft, and military prowess. These were the peoples who had settled in the Finger Lakes.

Their leaders included the great Mohawk prophet Dekanawida, and the eloquent Onondagan orator Hiawatha. Dekanawida's sagacity enabled the Iroquois to persevere in spite of seasonal food shortages and hostile Indian neighbors. Hiawatha was his spokesman. Together they worked for universal peace among the Indians. Their efforts resulted in the formation (*circa* 1452) of the League of the Iroquois or the Iroquois Confederacy. Through Hiawatha, Dekanawida taught that there is strength in union and that the Iroquois should strive for peace through reason and compromise, a plan remarkably similar in spirit to that of the original thirteen colonies when they drew up the Constitution and one that even invites comparison with the hopes of 1945, when the United Nations was established in San Francisco. The influence of the Confederacy was felt from the upper Hudson River to the southeastern shores of Lake Huron and Georgian Bay, and from the St Lawrence to the Chesapeake. At the height of the Confederacy's influence the English presence in America was for the most part a loose string of settlements along the Atlantic coast. Little was known about the interior regions of the New World and consequently only the most hearty and courageous of men dared venture as far west as the Finger Lakes.

The first white men to enter these wilderness lands were French explorers led by Samuel de Champlain in the years 1603–09. Fifty years later Jesuit missionaries, including Father Simon LeMoyne, attempted to colonize the region. Father LeMoyne is credited with the discovery of salt deposits in Onondaga Lake, a short distance from the present site of the city of Syracuse. Years later this discovery would provide the impetus for the first industry of the area.

For the next 150 years, as the English colonies prospered and expanded, the French and the British competed with the Iroquois for control of the lake country. The matter was settled in 1760 when the British defeated the French and their Indian allies and the same period marked the initial decline of the Iroquois Confederacy as a political force in America. By the end of the American Revolution in 1787 the great villages of the Iroquois had all but disappeared. Most of the territory which they had occupied was divided into 600-acre parcels and was awarded to US Army veterans as compensation for their military services.

The Finger Lakes region developed rapidly under the land-grant program. By 1804 the first salt works opened in Syracuse, creating jobs and other related industries. Two decades later the Erie Canal was completed in 1825. Construction of the canal was the most enterprising project attempted in 19th century America. Revolutionizing transportation between the Atlantic Ocean and the Great Lakes, the canal made economic history. It created towns, established cities, and made New York the 'Empire State'. Francis Kimball in *New York—the Canal State* (New York, 1937) said 'The Erie Canal rubbed Aladdin's lamp. America awoke, catching for the first time the wondrous vision of its own dimension and power.' By 1840 the railroads, speeding across the countryside, had made the canal obsolete and the Finger Lakes, once considered beyond the frontiers of human knowledge, had become a place of vigorous activity.

The lakes had been named by the Iroquois. They extend from 11 to 40 miles in length. Canandaigua, Keuka, Seneca, Cayuga, Owasco, and Skaneateles are the largest. The smaller lakes are Conesus, Hemlock, Canadice, Honeoye, and Otisco. The Onondagas tell us that their ancient tribesmen believed this area to be an enormous turtle and that the lakes were pools between the ridges in the creature's shell. Another popular version of the lake country's origin is that the lakes were caused by the imprint of the Creator's fingers as he blessed this favored land.

The Finger Lakes region abounds with important 'beginnings' that have affected the lives of untold numbers of Americans. The hills around the lakes were ideal for cultivating vineyards. The glens and waterfalls inspired an infant motion picture industry. Experiments were conducted in aviation, scientific farming, tool-making, sound-on-film, glass-making, and photography. These endeavors produced the first airplane pilot's license (Glen Curtiss, Hammondsport, 1911), the first US Navy seaplane ('Triad', Hammondsport, 1912), the first bonded winery in the US (Great Western, Hammondsport, 1860), the first successfully marketed adding machine (William Seward Burroughs, Auburn, 1892), the steel plow (Jethro Wood, Moravia, 1819), the first US fish hatchery (Caledonia, 1870), silent movies (Ithaca, 1915), the 'Bloomer' costume (Amelia Bloomer, Seneca Falls, 1849), and ice-cream sundaes (Red Cross Pharmacy, Ithaca, 1897).

The Book of Mormon was published in Palmyra in 1830. The Church of Jesus Christ of Latter-Day Saints believes that it was translated from the 'Golden Tablets' revealed to Joseph Smith by the Angel Moroni on Hill Cumorah. Smith's followers included Brigham Young who eventually succeeded Smith and led the Mormons to permanent settlement in the valley of the Great Salt Lake in Utah.

The first women's rights convention was convened by Elizabeth Cady Stanton in Seneca Falls in 1848. The first woman doctor in the United States, Elizabeth Blackwell, graduated from Geneva Medical College in 1849, and the first Memorial Day observance was celebrated in Waterloo in 1866. By presidential and congressional proclamation this Seneca County village is recognized as the birthplace of Memorial Day.

A native son of Auburn, William H. Seward, US Secretary of State under Presidents Lincoln and Johnson, negotiated with Russia for the purchase of Alaska in 1867. Referred to then as 'Seward's Folly', Alaska, twice the size of the State of Texas and rich in natural resources, was bought for $7,200,000. Seward was also a co-founder of the Republican Party in 1854. The Seward House has entertained such guests as Henry Clay, Daniel Webster, George Custer, and several Presidents of the United States. Brigham Young, who was a house painter and carpenter before he met Joseph Smith, reportedly worked on the construction of the Seward House.

Samuel Langhorne Clemens, the humorist and writer known to the world as Mark Twain, wrote chapters of *Tom Sawyer* (1876), *Huckleberry Finn* (1884), *The Prince and the Pauper* (1881), and many other famous stories in his summer home in Elmira.

Other distinguished individuals with ties to the Finger Lakes include Washington Irving, John D. Rockefeller, Harriet Tubman, Marcus Whitman, Millard Fillmore, Ezra Cornell, Jane Delano, Henry Wells, and William Fargo.

Various religious and mystic sects, apparently encouraged by the hospitality that the region afforded to nearly every new thought or idea, also had their origins around the Finger Lakes. Not all of them were to establish a place in history comparable to that of the Mormon Church. Soon after the Angel Moroni appeared to Joseph Smith, William Miller of Hampton persuaded thousands to prepare for the end of the world. Jemima Wilkinson, the 'Public Universal Friend', preached that she had been resurrected from the dead. In

Hydesville, the Fox sisters perfected the art of cracking the joints in their toes, to simulate mysterious rappings in their bedroom. These 'rappings' were then interpreted as messages from the dead.

The gift of imagination was not limited to the mystics. In 1869, in the village of Cardiff, a few miles south of Syracuse, two laborers digging a well on the farm of John Newell came upon the intact body of an enormous fossilized man, ten feet and four inches in height and weighing 2,290 pounds. A great controversy ensued as to whether or not the giant was a hoax. P.T. Barnum, the showman, less concerned with the authenticity of the creature than with the throngs of people interested in viewing it, offered Newell $60,000 for a three months' lease of the giant. Barnum was well known to Americans as the man who had given them a look at George Washington's 161-year-old nursemaid and at 'General Tom Thumb', a man who was 25 inches tall. When Newell refused, Barnum hired a Syracuse sculptor to duplicate the giant and then displayed the sculpture as 'the hoax of a hoax'. When Newell's representatives attempted to get an injunction against Barnum, the court ruled in favor of the showman.

At the height of these activities, the Finger Lakes Region was bluntly known as the 'Lunatic Fringe'. Today it is simply regarded as one of the most beautiful areas in America. As photographers, we have seen this beauty in the seasonal migration of wildlife, in the ruins of ancient campgrounds and in historic farmhouses, in hidden glens and valleys, and in the tranquillity of lake waters on quiet summer mornings. We found a land of myth and mystery, land of the Iroquois and of all the courageous men and women who followed them. Something of what we found was caught by our cameras and something of that is in this book.

Auburn, New York, 1984   JOHN FRANCIS McCARTHY

1 Glenora vineyards, Seneca Lake. Beginning with the first commercial grapes planted in 1829, more than 14,000 acres of land are now devoted to vineyards in the Finger Lakes region. The hills around Keuka Lake and other Finger Lakes are ideal for vineyards. Abundant shale gives the soil good drainage. The clear, deep waters of the glacier-gouged lakes temper the climate. The slow-warming lakes help to retard spring growth until frost danger is past; their warmth in later fall blankets the last ripening grapes on autumn nights.

2 Private road, Seneca Lake.

3 Peter Whitmer Cabin, Fayette; on 6 April 1830 Joseph Smith and
several of his followers met in this cabin to found what became the
Church of Jesus Christ of Latter Day Saints, commonly called the
Mormon Church. Orson Pratt, mathematician and philosopher, had
calculated that the day was exactly 1800 years after the Resurrection.

4 Fillmore Glen, Moravia.

5 Indian Exhibition, New York State Fair.

6 *(left)* Genesee Country Museum, Mumford.

7 Peter Whitmer Cabin, Fayette, interior.

8 *(left)* Millard Fillmore Cabin, Fillmore Glen State Park; a replica of the cabin in which the thirteenth President of the United States was born.

9 Taughannock Falls, near Ithaca, spills 215 feet in one of the longest straight-drop waterfalls east of the Mississippi River.

10 Genesee Country Museum, Mumford.

11 *(right)* Sonnenberg, Canandaigua, laid out in 1863, is one of the most magnificent Victorian garden estates ever created in America. Eight gardens, including rose, Japanese, Italian, rock, and colonial gardens, surround the mansion, which has seven restored period rooms.

12 Antique car show, Emerson Park. This annual event is held on th
north shore of Owasco Lake near the site of one of the first Indian
settlements in New York State.

13 Allan H. Treman State Marine Park, Ithaca.

14 Horse barn, New York State Fair, Syracuse. For ten days each year
'The Fair' is a showcase for the best of New York State.

15 Luchsinger's Farm on Onondaga Hill; registered offspring from
Isle of Jersey stock imported to Onondaga Hill about 1900.

16 *(left)* Otisco Lake.

17 Union Springs, Cayuga Lake; near Frontenac Island, one of two natural islands in the Finger Lakes.

18 Cayuga Museum of History and Art, Auburn; built in 1836 in the Greek Revival style, and donated by Theodore and Gertrude Case in 1936, for conversion to a museum.

19 *(right)* 'The Pines', Skaneateles, built by William Fulles in 1834, in the Ionic Greek Revival style.

20 'The Three Bears', Ovid. Construction of the largest and smallest building was completed in 1845. The buildings served as Court House, clerk's office and county jail.

21 Lincoln Hall, Cornell University, Ithaca.

22 Baker Dormitories, Cornell University, Ithaca.

23 Cornell University endowed the first chairs in American literature,
musicology, and American history, awarded the first degree in electrical
engineering, and established the first schools of hotel administration and
industrial and labor relations. Cornell was also the first major eastern
university to open its doors to women. Shown here is the McGraw
Tower.

24 *(left)* Roses at evening, Dresden.

25 Fireman's Field Days, Skaneateles.

26 Bathtub races, Moravia. This annual event highlights the celebration of Millard Fillmore Days and is billed as the only on-land bathtub race in America.

27 *(right)* Market Street, Corning.

28 Wells College, Aurora.

29 *(right)* The Seward House, Auburn, built in 1816-17 by Judge Elijah
Millar, Seward's father-in-law. Among those who worked on its construction
was Brigham Young, then a 16-year-old journeyman painter and carpenter.

30 Shadows at Sonnenberg.

31 *(right)* Livingston-Backus House, 1830,
Genesee Country Museum, Mumford.

32 Glen H. Curtiss Museum of Aviation and Local History,
Hammondsport. On 4 July 1908 Curtiss, in his first aeroplane, 'The
June Bug', made the first official, witnessed flight of one kilometer in
America, a feat which earned him Pilot's License Number One, issued
in 1911.

33 Prof. Walter H. Long, Director, the
Cayuga Museum of History and Art, with
one of the first sound-on-film projectors.

34 Foster-Tufts House, c. 1836, Genesee Country Museum, Mumford.

35 *(right)* Row houses, Geneva, overlooking Seneca Lake.

36 Women's Hall of Fame, Seneca Falls; a place where visitors learn of the tremendous contribution that women have made to America. Shown here are the Nobel Prize for literature, awarded in 1938 to Pearl Buck, the shoes of aviator Amelia Earhart (1897–1937), and relics of Mother Mary Seton who, in 1963, was the first American to be canonized by the Roman Catholic Church.

37 The Mark Twain Room, Elmira College. Elmira was the home of
Olivia Langdon, wife of Samuel Clemens, and it became his summer
home. While in Elmira, Clemens worked on *Huckleberry Finn, Tom
Sawyer, The Prince and the Pauper,* and many more stories that
contributed to his fame.

38 The Goddess Aurora, window in the main entrance of Wells College, Aurora; designed in 1897 by John LaFarge, the window represents Aurora heralding the dawn. The lakeside community was first named after the dawn by the Cayuga Indians because of the long eastern ridge that prolongs the sunrise.

39 *(right)* Country road, north of Auburn.

40 Ice-cream parlor, Corning.

41 Fence on South Street, Auburn.

42 Oakwood Cemetery, near Syracuse University.

43 *(right)* Off the road to Union Springs.

44 Venetian wine goblet, mid-16th century; The Corning Museum of Glass, Corning.

45 (*right*) Baccarat table (1878) and boat (1924); The Corning Museum of Glass, Corning.

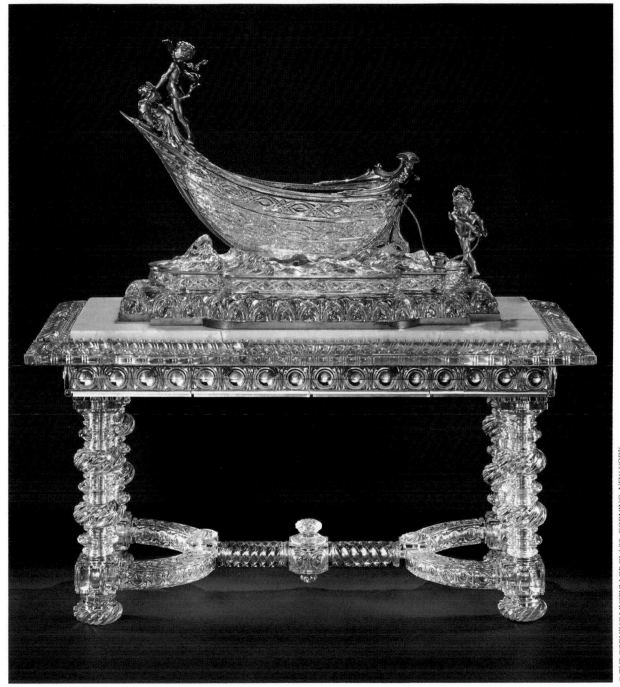

46 Pumpkins, Watkins Glen.

47 'The Krebs', Skaneateles, a landmark restaurant established in 1899.

48 & 49 Balloon races, Jamesville.

50 *(left)* Powers Road, Throop.

51 Montezuma National Wildlife Refuge
(see plate 70).

52 Looking north on Skaneateles Lake.

53 Winter south of Penn Yan.

54 *(left)* New Hope Mills has operated continuously since 1823. The 26-foot-overshot water-wheel is one of the largest in operation in the eastern United States. The machinery in use today was installed in 1892.

55 Chequagua Falls overlooking Main Street in Montour Falls.

56 *(left)* Owasco farmland.

57 The village of Skaneateles, said by William H. Seward to be located
on the shores of 'the most beautiful body of water in the world.'

58 Foster Road, near Marcellus.

59 Winter, high above Keuka Lake.

60 'Great Western', Hammondsport, first (1860) bonded winery in the
United States.

61 *(right)* Sunday morning in Mennonite country, Penn Yan.

62 *(left)* Rose Hill, a Greek Revival mansion, built in 1839, reflects the social and cultural environment that prevailed in Geneva during the 1840s and provides a rare view of early nineteenth-century America.

63 Owasco Stockade; replica of a hut of *circa* A.D. 300. The Owasco Indians were farmers who had evolved a highly complex community life. The Iroquois, who arrived in the area in the fourteenth-century, were the inheritors of this great Owasco culture.

64 Bluff Point, Keuka Lake; aerial view of Skyline Drive. The Y-shape
of the lake is due to the fact that it was once the confluence of two
rivers, both flowing south into what is now the Susquehanna River
basin.
65 *(right)* Country road, west of Auburn.

66 Rose at Christmas; this area south of Lake Ontario is noted for apple orchards and cobblestone houses, and is also home to the Hill Cumorah Pageant and the Apple Blossom Festival.

67 *(right)* Moravia; Millard Fillmore, thirteenth President of the United States, was born near this village in the Owasco Valley, where John D. Rockefeller spent his youth, and where Jethro Wood had invented the first cast-iron plow in 1819.

68 *(left)* Scott, south of Skaneateles Lake, in winter.

69 Rose Post Office.

70 Montezuma National Wildlife Refuge, at the north end of Cayuga Lake. The largest concentration of water-fowl occurs during migration in April and October. On their journey between Chesapeake Bay and Hudson Bay Canada geese and ducks stop at Montezuma to rest, feed and nest.

71 *(right)* South Street, Auburn

72 *(left)* Going towards Otisco from Skaneateles.

73 Lighthouse, Sodus Point; noted for its excellent year-round fishing
for coho salmon and lake, brown, and rainbow trout.

74 Christmas Tree lighting ceremony, Clinton Square, Syracuse.

75 Union Springs at dusk.

76 Barge canal lock, Mays Point. The Seneca was the name of the first boat that traveled the Erie Canal from Buffalo to New York City in 1825. The journey took nine days to travel the 525-mile longest canal in the world.

77 *(right)* Owasco Lake, near Moravia.

78 *(left)* Spring planting on Owasco Lake. In 1835 Scottish immigrant John Johnston introduced a method of draining agricultural lands by burying ceramic tile. Johnston was also a pioneer in such practices as the use of lime and plaster, the surface application of manure, the purchase of oil feed for cattle and sheep, and the early cultivation of hay.

79 William H. Seward's grave in Fort Hill Cemetery, Auburn.

80 *(left)* George Eastman House, Rochester, home of the International
Museum of Photography.

81 Garden view of the George Eastman House, Rochester.

82 Livingston-Backus House, Genesee Country Museum, Mumsford.

83 *(right)* South Main Street, Geneva, near the campus of Hobart and William Smith Colleges.

84 Otisco Lake.